RELATIONAL INTELLIGENCE

Nurturing Connections and Building Meaningful Relationships (2023 Guide for Beginners)

Derick Steele

First edition

This book was professionally typeset on Reedsy.
Find out more at reedsy.com

Contents

Introduction

The way individuals behave or respond in different situations, circumstances, and social gatherings can have either positive or negative implications. This behavior reflects a person's relational intelligence, which enables one to understand the needs of people around them, even without direct communication. Our intellectual capabilities allow us to grasp the needs of ourselves and others. However, truly knowing oneself is a complex process, and no one can fully comprehend their capabilities or have a complete understanding of themselves.

Many people, millions in fact, lack self-awareness and struggle to identify their life goals. As a result, they may be alive but not truly living, limited in their experiences due to this lack of self-awareness. Knowing oneself goes beyond recognizing personal traits or emotional well-being. It is an ongoing learning journey, as personal growth never truly ends.

Certain traits, like shyness, have both positive and negative aspects. Shyness can be debilitating if not managed healthily. Studies suggest that introverts may possess higher verbal intelligence and exhibit greater intelligence and giftedness. While they may excel in listening and retaining information, they might find it challenging to perform in socially demanding work environments or take on leadership roles. Traits like extreme shyness and introverted tendencies can hinder people from reaching their full potential as they fear judgment and criticism. This often stems from a lack of confidence, self-esteem, and potential insecurity, which can be influenced by various factors.

These characteristics are just a few examples of factors that hinder people from connecting with others and establishing trust in personal, social, or professional relationships. They impose limitations and challenges, especially when combined with anxiety, emotional trauma, certain psychological traits, or behavioral issues. Developing social skills is crucial for unlocking one's true potential and overcoming these obstacles in various aspects of life.

Having certain traits might lead to communication difficulties that can hinder your ability to handle daily tasks, putting you at a clear disadvantage. However, it is possible to develop your relational intelligence and improve your interpersonal skills and undesirable traits. This doesn't mean changing who you are, but rather evolving and dealing with people, work, and life in a more constructive way.

By building relational intelligence, you can confront reality and overcome obstacles that hold you back. Achieving a balance between your personal and professional life, forming better connections, and nurturing relationships beyond what you thought possible becomes attainable. This growth will enhance your career and leadership abilities, as you commit to constant improvement and learning from your experiences. Developing relational intelligence also reduces sensitivity to others' behaviors, equips you to manage stress, enhances your communication skills, and provides self-awareness to meet your needs effectively. You'll also learn to fine-tune your behavioral responses to stress.

Imagine having the ability to manage your stress responses and transform the way you approach, experience, and conclude each day. With this newfound skill, you can confidently face challenges and seize opportunities in your daily life. Ultimately, you'll discover a sense of balance that allows you to live life to the fullest.

Relational Intelligence for the Win

Establishing connections with the people in our lives, whether they are family, friends, colleagues, or new acquaintances, is crucial for personal growth. Some individuals may be used to a solitary approach or minimal social interactions and might not see the relevance of connecting with more people. However, embracing change and continuous growth are essential for wisdom and progress.

Similar to how we learn essential skills like walking, talking, and driving, we must also focus on further personal development. This doesn't mean being overly critical of ourselves, but it's unfortunate that many people neglect their personal growth entirely. Just as we put effort into our work to achieve results, connecting with others requires similar dedication. Even if someone's personality may not align with the concept of networking, they can still learn how to connect with others by adjusting their habits, respecting differing opinions, handling disagreements constructively, and establishing mutual trust, especially in the workplace.

Establishing trust with your team is vital for excelling in personal relationships and work. It can lead to better performance and job satisfaction, something not everyone can claim to have these days. Our responses to people and situations can hold us back from reaching our goals and dreams. Self-development and growth are closely intertwined, and if social skills are lacking or if we recognize that we are hindering ourselves, it's essential to make adjustments.

Relational intelligence, unlike emotional intelligence, focuses on forming connections to solve problems rather than solely managing emotions. In the modern workplace, continuous growth and engagement in diverse workplace cultures are expected from employees to contribute to business performance. Companies now prioritize certain values to support their identities, and employees face new challenges accordingly. Therefore, it is impractical to lack connections with coworkers and clients. Developing relational intelligence is crucial for leadership growth as well. Leaders who cannot connect with their team or understand their clients may lead their companies to failure.

A leader's ability to handle people directly impacts how their employees or team members operate. Often, team members wait for their leader to earn their trust before giving their best performance. Imagine the potential achievements if you can successfully connect with your team. This can be achieved by understanding the differences between conflict and communication and applying relevant principles at work, such as self-awareness and accountability. Building trust with your team allows you to cultivate their expertise and commitment to the business, leading to a competitive advantage.

Improving your relational intelligence can benefit you in various roles, whether as an employee, team player, leader, spouse, parent, family member, or friend. It requires self-acceptance, clarity, and hard work. Developing yourself not only enhances your interactions with others, makes you a better leader, and strengthens relationships but also provides you with a competitive edge. When you know yourself and have clear goals, you become more in control and capable of devising strategies to achieve success in this fast-paced and competitive world, unlike many others who lack direction and clarity.

Opt for a proactive approach rather than being passive. To enhance your relational intelligence, observe and learn from the people around you. This involves not only engaging in comfortable conversations but also initiating them. Improving your ability to connect with others requires practice in expressing your thoughts, sharing opinions, and actively participating in discussions, such as providing input during meetings. Avoiding the fear of expressing yourself will only hinder your growth. Stepping out of your comfort zone and engaging in dialogues instead of monologues is essential for personal development.

Recognize the significance of self-awareness in your life. Self-awareness entails having conscious knowledge of your character and emotions. Those who are confident, self-assured, and opinionated tend to possess higher levels of self-awareness compared to others. Developing self-awareness is crucial for advancing in your career, nurturing relationships, and overall life improvement. Understanding ourselves empowers us to make positive changes, focusing on strengths, and working on weaknesses. Assessing your self-awareness can be done by examining how kindly you treat yourself. Negative self-talk and limiting beliefs impede growth. By practicing self-awareness, acknowledging your thoughts and emotions, you can gain a more objective perspective of yourself and others, identifying areas for improvement and developing strategies for personal growth.

Rather than just hearing, actively listen and be attentive in conversations. Communication involves more than just words; it includes subtle hints, body language, and emotional cues. Paying attention to these hidden dynamics allows you to salvage potentially negative conversations and adjust your communication style accordingly. Knowing how to talk to different people and striking the right balance between sharing and holding back in conversations is crucial. Mutual respect is fostered when both parties listen attentively, consider each other's perspectives, and pause to understand the true meaning behind the words. Establishing trust with coworkers, family members, friends, and even strangers is facilitated through such attentive and respectful communication.

Be fully present in the current moment. In our daily lives, various distractions keep us from being fully present in the moment. Often, we may appear physically alert, but internally, we are disconnected from ourselves and the people around us. Two main factors contributing to this disconnection are technology and work demands, especially for millennials. The constant urge to keep up with online activities leads us to overlook the things right in front of us. For our generation, staying connected with others requires practice, including disconnecting from excessive technology use and work hours. To counter this, we can practice being present in the moment and find ways to reconnect with those we may have lost touch with, such as family and friends. Engaging in activities that refresh our minds and promote relaxation, like hobbies, reading, journaling, physical exercise, and meditation, also help foster a present-focused mindset.

A welcoming attitude towards others is vital alongside being present. Imagine engaging in a conversation with someone while continuously checking your phone for notifications and messages. Such behavior may unintentionally signal disinterest to the other person, making them feel unheard and undervalued. To approach others with a welcoming attitude, it is essential to switch off digitally when in the presence of others, making them feel valued and cared for. A simple text message or phone call to check in on people also demonstrates thoughtfulness and consideration. Planning to meet up with close friends, family members, and acquaintances is an excellent way to strengthen relationships and build trust with others.

Why Master Social Skills?

Social skills encompass the ability to communicate effectively with others through verbal and non-verbal means, including gestures, appearance, and body language. Not everyone has developed these skills to the same extent, and some individuals struggle to interact effectively, often limiting their communication to only necessary or familiar circles. Whether one is considered shy, introverted, or highly advanced in social interactions, there is always room for improvement in how we engage with others.

A lack of social skills can significantly impact daily life, including work performance and navigating public settings. Engaging with a group or meeting new people can be challenging without adequate communication abilities, as it plays a crucial role in establishing mutual trust. Even in relationships built on a strong foundation, effective communication remains essential. While it may seem daunting for shy or introverted individuals to develop social skills, the key to overcoming this is consistent practice.

Unfortunately, today's generation is experiencing a decline in quality face-to-face social interactions. With increased screen time due to smartphones, TVs, tablets, and computers, there is a concerning rise in depression and self-harm cases among teenagers in the United States. Practicing social skills is crucial in fostering interaction and dialogue among teens and young adults, promoting the initiation of innovative ideas, problem-solving, and building a supportive network of friends. Social interaction contributes to better emotional, mental, and social well-being, reducing feelings of loneliness and isolation. The more someone interacts with others, the happier and more content they tend to feel.

Beyond personal relationships, social skills also play a significant role in sustaining work relations and business deals. They support a successful career by enabling effective communication, teamwork, and seizing opportunities. Poor social skills can hinder maintaining conversations, working with colleagues, and obtaining potential opportunities. Developing social skills can propel one's career and achievements, providing the confidence to communicate, share ideas, and take necessary actions in professional settings. Even if a highly social demeanor may not seem crucial for career advancement, having strong social skills can be the key to success in the business world or when taking risks in entrepreneurial endeavors.

Social connections play a significant role in our well-being. Having strong social relationships leads to better health and a longer life, which is something everyone desires, as time is highly valued in today's fast-paced world. While modern innovations and scientific advancements aim to make our lives more efficient, many daily activities still waste our time. While some individuals may find fulfillment in spending time alone, social interaction remains an essential aspect of human life. Developing social skills is crucial, even to some extent, as they are necessary for improving existing relationships, creating new connections, and establishing work relations. Communication and interaction are integral to success, whether in personal or professional spheres. Inability to approach people and engage in effective communication can hinder personal growth and career advancement. Building a large social circle provides opportunities for personal and professional development, opening doors to more connections and prospects.

Developed social skills allow individuals to express their emotions effectively, which can be challenging for many people. Being open about feelings fosters connections and makes others more comfortable engaging in conversations. Effective communication of emotions allows for better understanding among individuals, facilitating stronger relationships. By developing social skills, one gains the ability to convey emotions clearly, creating a positive impact on interactions with others.

Steps to Becoming Friendly

1. **Embrace change in your behavior.**

In today's world, the emphasis on being true to yourself and embracing individuality is essential for personal growth. However, becoming too comfortable with where you are in life and with yourself can hinder progress. Just because you feel at ease does not mean there is no room for improvement. While it may seem undesirable to make yourself uncomfortable, many people fall into this trap. Consider the scenario where social situations make you uncomfortable, leading you to avoid interactions with others. Although it might provide temporary relief, does it truly foster personal growth? If being more sociable can benefit you, then it's essential to challenge yourself and engage in various social situations. Overcoming social anxiety is not easy, as it is not something that can be instantly resolved. Anxiety often hinders the development of social skills due to fear of communicating with strangers, insecurities, and the dread of failure and judgment from others.

- **Take gradual steps in social situations.**

If you find yourself uncomfortable in large gatherings, don't feel pressured to dive into the deep end right away. Instead, start small and work your way up. As an introvert, small talk might be daunting, but it's a crucial skill to develop for social growth. Begin by engaging in basic conversations with acquaintances, servers, or even participating in a low-pressure activity. Gradually increase the level of difficulty as you become more comfortable.

· **Educate yourself on social skills.**

Self-development involves continuous learning. To evolve beyond your current reality, it's essential to consume new knowledge through reading books or surrounding yourself with people who can impart wisdom. Reading about self-development and social skills can provide valuable insights into initiating and engaging in meaningful conversations. However, simply acquiring knowledge is not enough; taking action on what you learn is vital to harness the power of this information.

· **Encourage others to share about themselves.**

Notice that many people enjoy talking about their experiences and thoughts. Embracing this trait allows you to learn more about them. For shy or introverted individuals, this can be both advantageous and challenging. While you may prefer less conversation, creating a space for others to share can build trust and connection. By actively listening and asking questions, you show genuine interest in their stories, making them feel valued and comfortable. This approach allows you to develop social skills gradually and foster meaningful connections without the pressure of speaking excessively.

· **Start conversations with compliments.**

If you find yourself unsure of what to say or how to begin a conversation, a compliment can be an effective icebreaker. By offering a genuine compliment to a coworker or friend about their work, appearance, attire, or even possessions, you show that you are friendly, selfless, and open to communication. This gesture makes the other person feel good, creating a positive association with you and laying the foundation for a constructive personal or professional relationship.

- **Pay attention to non-verbal cues.**

Communication comprises both verbal and non-verbal elements. While people often focus on verbal communication, they tend to overlook non-verbal signals. Neglecting to read these cues can lead to misunderstandings, conflicts, or disliking between individuals. Some people excel at verbal communication but struggle with interpreting social cues, such as eye contact and body language. For instance, if someone appears uncomfortable discussing a certain topic, continuing to talk about it can deter them from engaging in further conversations with you.

- **Cultivate approachable manners.**

Displaying good manners makes you more approachable, attracting people towards initiating conversations with you. Practicing politeness, expressing gratitude with words like "please," "thank you," and "you're welcome," can win people over. Additionally, performing favors for friends, family, and co-workers can enhance your likability and demonstrate your considerate nature. Going the extra mile for others sets a positive tone for how you treat them and reflects positively on your character.

- **Establish regular targets.**

To enhance your sociability and social skills, it is essential to track your progress consistently. This is especially crucial for those who feel uninterested in meeting new people or tend to avoid social situations. It may be tempting to cancel plans or convince yourself that you don't need to work on your social skills. That's why setting regular goals, both small and significant, becomes vital. Holding yourself accountable to achieve these goals, such as attending a social event, can accelerate your progress. Writing down your goals and checking them off one by one can foster positivity and enjoyment in the journey, transforming tasks you once disliked into purposeful steps towards growth.

· **Recognize and overcome negative thoughts.**

In your journey of self-improvement, negative thoughts can act as stumbling blocks. If you entertain these thoughts, they may persist and hinder your efforts to develop your social skills. It is crucial to maintain a positive attitude and challenge these thoughts. Negative thoughts like feeling awkward, fearing embarrassment, or believing you are incapable of effective communication are common but can be addressed. Replace self-doubt with empowering affirmations, such as "I can," and take actionable steps to prove these thoughts wrong.

· **Seek support through group engagement.**

If you ever feel alone in your struggles with communication or lack the courage to step out of your comfort zone, remember that you are not the only one facing such challenges. Many individuals experience shyness, introversion, anxiety, and insecurities that lead to avoidance of social interactions. Consider joining a support group or finding like-minded individuals who share similar social challenges. Together, you can combat fears and insecurities, encouraging each other to evolve and become more sociable. This support network will hold you accountable to achieve your goals and celebrate collective progress towards enhanced social skills.

Emotional Intelligence: Get to Know Yourself

Emotional intelligence encompasses the skill of managing emotions while also navigating interpersonal relationships adeptly. It involves responding maturely to the emotions of others and should not be confused with relational intelligence, which focuses on staying connected during tasks. High emotional intelligence, often measured by EQ, enables individuals to be more aware of their surroundings, including the emotions of people around them. Those with developed emotional intelligence can recognize, understand, and effectively handle various emotions, both their own and those of others. This quality is particularly crucial for leaders as it influences their responses to stress and challenges. A leader with high emotional intelligence is more likely to handle difficult situations constructively, fostering a positive team environment.

Leadership emotional intelligence can be categorized into five main subtypes, while personal emotional intelligence encompasses four main types.

1.Personal Emotional Intelligence

● Emotional Self-Control This aspect involves effectively managing impulsive reactions and emotions, adopting healthy emotional responses, and demonstrating commitment by adapting to changing circumstances.
● Empathy and Social Awareness Social awareness encompasses empathy, which is the ability to comprehend and share the emotions of others. When

socially aware, you can easily pick up on social cues, understand people's emotions, concerns, and needs, and navigate social situations comfortably. Additionally, you grasp the dynamics of power within groups or organizations.

● Self-Awareness Recognizing your emotions and understanding how they impact your thoughts and behaviors is essential. Self-awareness enables you to identify your strengths and weaknesses and maintain self-confidence, irrespective of any perceived limitations.

● Relationship Management This skill involves initiating, cultivating, and sustaining relationships. With effective relationship management, you can communicate clearly and inspire others to work individually or collaboratively. Moreover, you handle conflicts adeptly.

Individual emotional intelligence significantly influences various aspects of life, including academic and professional performance, physical and mental well-being, relationships, and social interactions. It can either propel you forward or hinder your progress significantly, making it crucial to work on its improvement. Unfortunately, this vital skill is often neglected in traditional education settings, leaving individuals without the knowledge and tools to enhance their emotional intelligence effectively.

Emotional intelligence has a profound impact on various aspects of life:

1. School or Work Performance: High emotional intelligence enables smoother navigation of social challenges in the workplace, making it easier to lead and motivate both oneself and others. It contributes to career success and fosters a growth mindset. Conversely, low emotional intelligence can hinder dealing with difficult tasks and people, leading to a fixed mindset.

2. Physical and Mental Health: Poorly developed emotional intelligence can lead to difficulty managing stress, resulting in serious physical and mental health issues. Physically, it increases the risk of heart attacks, strokes, hypertension, and aging, while causing fatigue, immune suppression, and infertility. Mentally, it can lead to uncontrolled

emotions, contributing to depression and anxiety. Developing emotional intelligence leads to greater happiness, better health, and improved relationships.

3. Relationships: In personal life, nurturing and developing relationships require effort. High emotional intelligence facilitates effective communication and sustainable relationships in both personal and professional domains.

4. Social Intelligence: While achieving complete emotional awareness is challenging, improving emotional intelligence allows better reading of others. It helps recognize who is beneficial or detrimental to your well-being and understand others' interests and disinterest in you. Developing emotional intelligence also aids in reducing stress, balancing the nervous system through social interactions, and increasing contentment with oneself.

2.Leadership Emotional Intelligence:

Self-awareness: Developing emotional intelligence enhances self-awareness, helping leaders understand their feelings, strengths, and weaknesses. Recognizing one's limitations and strengths is vital for continuous growth and improvement. Keeping a journal and acknowledging emotions can promote humility and constructive reactions to negative feelings.

Motivation: Higher emotional intelligence drives increased motivation to achieve high standards in work and reach goals. Reflect on the reasons for job choice and find ways to increase job satisfaction and fulfillment. Maintain optimism and hope in both positive and negative situations to foster progress and resilience.

Self-regulation: Effective self-regulation prevents impulsive decision-making and categorizing people based on stereotypes. Leaders with emotional intelligence have control over their emotions, take personal accountability, and commit to work responsibilities. Correct values, if necessary, accept consequences, and practice calmness to handle stress positively.

Empathy: Empathy is crucial for leaders, and higher emotional intelligence correlates with greater empathy. Being empathetic enables leaders to support others' development, challenge their teams constructively, provide helpful feedback, and treat individuals with respect and value. Viewing situations from others' perspectives and paying attention to body language can improve empathy.

Social skills: Developed social skills are essential for effective leadership and communication. Leaders must handle both good and bad news, manage change and conflicts, and foster a positive work environment. Improving emotional intelligence enhances social skills, including conflict resolution, verbal communication, providing feedback, and showing appreciation for team members' efforts.

Take Control of Your Feelings

We hold complete control over our emotions because we are the architects of our lives. Every decision we make, including how we react to people, work, and experiences, is within our power. Although life may present various outcomes, we ultimately determine how we feel about them. When faced with upsetting comments or situations, we have the choice of how to respond. While it's natural to experience hurt, anger, sadness, or disappointment, learning to manage these emotions positively can have a significant impact on our future responses and feelings. By understanding that we can always take charge of how we feel and react, we become better equipped to handle conflicts or avoid them altogether. This newfound awareness allows us to mend strained relationships, maintain healthy ones, make wiser choices, enjoy more meaningful interactions, and prioritize self-care.

To gain control over our emotions, it is essential to develop our regulation skills, which significantly contribute to our overall well-being. When emotions dominate us, we lose control of our lives, hindering our progress in various aspects. A sense of stagnation or unfulfillment can harm our emotional, mental, and physical well-being. Therefore, focusing on our emotional health becomes crucial. Unfortunately, many people, especially men, tend to neglect this aspect. Society often encourages men to suppress emotions rather than deal with them positively, leading to detrimental consequences for their well-being. Both men and women should embrace the importance of managing emotions constructively.

How To Enhance Emotional Regulation

● **Assess the impact of personal emotions.**

Experiencing intense emotions can have both positive and negative effects on your life. While it can add vibrancy and excitement, it may also lead to overwhelming feelings when something remarkable or distressing occurs. It is crucial to understand how you react to these emotions and whether you can manage them effectively. Take the time to evaluate the impact of your emotions on your daily life. Consider both the positive and negative aspects of intense emotions and make a note of situations that tend to overwhelm you. This self-awareness will help you recognize any issues and take appropriate steps to address them. Signs of poor emotional regulation may include conflicts in relationships, difficulty relating to others, work or school dissatisfaction, emotional or physical outbursts, and reliance on substances to cope with emotions.

● **Opt for regulation instead of repression.**

Rather than suppressing your emotions, it is essential to learn how to handle them in a healthy manner. Choosing emotional regulation over repression allows you to avoid impulsive responses to your feelings, whether intentional or unintentional. Repressing emotions prevents you from acknowledging and expressing them, which can lead to various mental and physical issues, such as depression, anxiety, insomnia, increased stress, substance abuse, and physical tension. Overall, it can significantly harm your well-being. Instead of avoiding emotions, strive for a balanced approach between expressing too little and too much. Embrace your emotions and find constructive ways to manage and express them.

● Acknowledge and embrace your emotions.

Taking control of your emotions begins with recognizing and accepting what you are feeling, which is often overlooked. Without identifying your emotions, it becomes challenging to address them constructively. By acknowledging your feelings, consider the following questions: What emotions are you experiencing? What triggered these feelings? Are there multiple explanations that could shed light on your emotions and their causes? How do you want to respond to your feelings? Can you approach your emotions in a more positive manner? Answering these questions truthfully and jotting down your responses, whether positive or negative, allows you to recognize patterns and practice more positive reactions to situations and feelings. Acceptance of your emotions is vital before you can move forward and handle them in a constructive way.

● Maintain a mood journal.

Writing down your feelings can be a powerful tool in overcoming obstacles. Keeping a mood journal enables you to review and contemplate your emotions rather than just thinking about them and forgetting. By documenting your feelings, you can identify any disruptive thoughts and trace the origins of your emotions back to their underlying causes. Regularly reflecting on your feelings empowers you to engage in self-therapy without seeking external guidance. This practice helps you identify triggers and address them productively. To maximize the benefits of journaling, make it a daily habit or document your feelings twice a day to gain a comprehensive understanding of your emotions. Keep your journal with you at all times, so you can record overwhelming emotions and learn to cope better the next time they arise.

● Practice intentional breathing.

Slowing down and focusing on your breath doesn't eliminate emotions, but it creates space for reflection on your day and potential concerns. Intentional breathing can signal your brain to adjust the parasympathetic part of your nervous system, inducing a sense of calmness and reducing your heart rate and digestion pace. It also boosts the sympathetic nervous system, releasing serotonin, a hormone that promotes well-being. Proper breathing is not only beneficial for stress management, but it also detoxifies your body and promotes relaxation. Being relaxed enhances your ability to tackle challenges with a positive mindset. Incorporate deep breathing exercises into your routine to effectively manage your emotions. When feeling overwhelmed, practice slow deep breaths through your nose, briefly hold the breath, and exhale through your mouth while focusing on a positive mantra, such as "I will have a good day" or "I am feeling completely relaxed."

● **Choose appropriate times to express yourself and practice meditation.**
While it is healthy to express your emotions, it is crucial to recognize the

appropriate moments for doing so. Reacting impulsively when feeling upset or emotional is rarely beneficial. Being mindful of your surroundings helps you determine when it is suitable to respond to your feelings or when it is better to take a moment to process them before reacting. Incorporating meditation into your routine can assist you in managing intense emotions. Meditation enhances self-awareness and deepens your understanding of your feelings and experiences, enabling you to express yourself only in necessary and suitable situations.

● **Find enjoyment and manage stress.**

Creating a distance from intense emotions allows for more rational responses. Distancing yourself may involve physically leaving a negative or uncomfortable situation or mentally diverting your attention. Avoiding emotions entirely is not helpful, so taking breaks and engaging in enjoyable activities can help manage stress in positive ways. Consider taking weekends to relax, going for a walk, watching a movie, spending time with loved ones, or indulging in self-care activities like a spa day or treating yourself to something luxurious.

● **Seek support without fear.**

Seeking professional help can be instrumental in gaining control over your emotions. While not everyone may be open to therapy, it can provide valuable support. Experiencing mood swings or emotional dysregulation is common, but persistent emotional issues may require medical guidance. Therapy can help you work through underlying concerns, unresolved issues, or trauma, as well as manage mental health conditions such as bipolar disorder or personality disorders. There should be no shame in seeking help, as everyone faces mental challenges at some point in their lives. A therapist can help explore factors contributing to emotional dysregulation, navigate distressing feelings, address mood swings, learn emotional regulation techniques, and improve emotional expression.

Healing from Emotional Trauma

Emotional trauma can significantly impact a person's emotional intelligence and overall well-being. Such trauma may arise from experiences like bullying, betrayal, emotional or physical abuse, or other events that affect one's emotional response to life. Dealing with emotional trauma is essential to improving emotional intelligence, even though it may feel overwhelming or challenging. It is common for individuals to either take time to recover from trauma or unconsciously suppress it into their subconscious, avoiding it for years. However, taking action and implementing self-help strategies are crucial steps towards healing and moving past the trauma.

Overcoming emotional trauma is not a simple task, as it can create stress and impair one's sense of security. This trauma may lead to feelings of helplessness, difficulty managing emotions, anxiety, and haunting memories. It can also erode trust in others and hinder the ability to live life fully, as triggers from the trauma persist even when trying to suppress them. Revisiting or thinking about the emotional experience can trigger fear and distress.

Several factors can lead to emotional and psychological trauma, including one-time events like accidents, violence, injuries, or childhood experiences, ongoing stress from life-threatening illnesses, negative environments, bullying, neglect, or abuse, and unexpected occurrences like surgeries, loss of a loved one, breakups, humiliation, or disappointment.

Coping with emotional trauma presents direct and indirect challenges that individuals must learn to manage to live without constraints. Healing from trauma requires finding a way to make peace with it and allowing oneself to heal fully. By taking the necessary steps to cope with and heal from emotional trauma, individuals can improve their emotional intelligence and overall well-being.

Coping with Childhood Trauma and Potential Future Trauma

Throughout our lives, we encounter various losses, unique experiences, and stressors that may cause emotional trauma. However, it is essential to approach dealing with these challenges with courage rather than fear. Psychological symptoms of trauma can manifest as disbelief, denial, confusion, impaired concentration, shock, anger, mood swings, irritability, fear, anxiety, guilt, self-blame, shame, hopelessness, disconnection, loneliness, sadness, or numbness, often leading to withdrawing from others. Additionally, physical symptoms may include fatigue, insomnia, nightmares, heightened startle response, rapid heartbeat, difficulty concentrating, muscle tension, aches, and agitation.

To heal from emotional trauma, it is crucial to work through your memories and address any triggers that may evoke upsetting emotional responses. If dealing with trauma becomes overwhelming or worsens over time, it could be indicative of Post-Traumatic Stress Disorder (PTSD), which may require professional therapy to process and heal from the emotional trauma. Similarly, when experiencing loss or a sense of insecurity, it is essential to go through the grieving process as a means of healing and finding closure. Embracing these healing processes can help individuals cope with childhood trauma and prepare for potential future challenges with strength and resilience.

Recovery from Trauma

1. Engage in Physical Activity: Trauma can disrupt your physical balance, leading to hyperarousal and fear. To cope with this, it is essential to become active and start exercising. Regular physical activity helps burn off adrenaline and triggers the release of endorphins, which aids in repairing the nervous system. Aim for at least 30 minutes of exercise, four to five days a week. You can try rhythmic exercises such as walking, hiking, running, swimming, and dancing. Activities like boxing, yoga, Pilates, martial arts, and weightlifting that involve rhythmic breathing can also be beneficial.

2. Avoid Isolation: Although it may seem natural to isolate yourself when dealing with trauma, isolating yourself can hinder the healing process.

Instead, connect with others to promote faster recovery. Spending too much time alone can be detrimental to your emotional well-being. Surround yourself with supportive people who provide a sense of engagement, acceptance, and understanding, even if you don't discuss the trauma explicitly. Don't hesitate to seek support from trustworthy individuals who can help you work through your emotions effectively. Engaging in social activities with friends or family can offer a healthy escape and create a sense of normalcy. Additionally, consider joining a support group for trauma survivors to gain perspective and learn from others' experiences. Building new connections or rekindling old friendships can also facilitate healing by providing fresh experiences and perspectives.

3. Practice Nervous System Self-Regulation: When you feel overwhelmed, agitated, or emotionally out of control, it may seem challenging to manage your feelings constructively. However, you can overcome these limiting beliefs by engaging in mindful breathing exercises. Take 60 controlled breaths to bring yourself to a calmer state. Another effective approach is to focus on sensory experiences that soothe you mentally and physically, providing instant stress relief. Ground yourself in the present moment by sitting still and appreciating the simple things around you, such as nature or the beauty of your surroundings. By allowing yourself to genuinely experience and acknowledge your emotions, you can find realistic and sustainable ways to cope with them.

4. Prioritize Self-Care: Taking care of your health is crucial for effectively dealing with emotional trauma. Ensure you get enough sleep, aiming for 7 to 9 hours each night to maintain emotional balance. Avoid alcohol and drugs, as they can worsen trauma symptoms. Minimize stress by practicing self-care activities that nurture your well-being. Maintaining a balanced diet will also contribute to your overall emotional strength, enabling you to manage emotional trauma more effectively. By looking after yourself, you will build the resilience needed to overcome emotional challenges without being hindered by them.

Enhance Self-Esteem and Confidence

Low confidence is a clear indication of underdeveloped emotional intelligence, which can hinder your progress in both professional and personal aspects of life. It might prevent you from excelling in your career, securing job opportunities, or participating effectively in meetings and discussions. When self-esteem is lacking, you may constantly face uncertainty, holding you back from reaching your full potential.

For individuals struggling with low self-esteem, stepping out of their comfort zone and speaking up can be an enormous challenge. Although others might encourage them to do so, building confidence takes time and consistent effort. Comparing oneself to seemingly confident individuals can lead to feelings of envy, as the journey towards comfort in attention-seeking situations isn't simple.

Improving emotional intelligence requires addressing insecurities, practicing self-care, and working towards greater self-assurance. Self-acceptance is a vital component, as it not only helps you become more confident but also demonstrates to others that you are secure in yourself. By cultivating self-esteem and confidence, you will experience increased career success, satisfaction, and potentially higher earnings.

Moreover, social interactions will become more manageable, even if you lack natural social skills. You'll find it easier to navigate social settings and build meaningful personal relationships.

As your self-confidence grows, you'll naturally become more positive and optimistic. Taking on new challenges and stepping outside your comfort zone will no longer seem daunting, allowing you to focus on your goals and embrace opportunities with ease. Ultimately, boosting self-esteem and confidence can lead to a more fulfilling and successful life.

Some individuals believe that excessive self-confidence can be mistaken for arrogance, but this is not necessarily the case. Confidence itself does not automatically make you appear arrogant. However, when confidence becomes excessive, displayed aggressively, and persists all the time, it can have negative consequences. People's perceptions of your self-confidence, whether it is too low or too high, can influence how they treat and respect you, including colleagues and superiors. Overly high self-confidence may also indicate imbalanced emotional intelligence, which can lead to disruptions in various aspects of life. Striking a balance in self-esteem and confidence is crucial in gauging whether your emotional intelligence is well-adjusted and knowing when to adapt your approach accordingly.

To become more self-aware, it is essential to recognize your strengths and weaknesses and identify areas for potential improvement. Both self-awareness and confidence are valuable competencies that contribute to better self-perception.

If you wish to assess your level of self-confidence, consider the following:

- In times of conflict, do you feel singled out and defensive?
- Are you the first to voice your opinions in discussions?
- Do you dominate conversations without actively listening to others?
- Can you express your viewpoints confidently and without hesitation?
- Do you tend to take strong positions on matters frequently?
- Do you tend to shut down further discussions to support your stance?
- Are you willing to stand firm or easily yield when faced with aggression from others?

After careful reflection, you can determine if you lack confidence or if your confidence is bordering on arrogance. True confidence allows you to strike a healthy balance between your needs and those of others, whether in a professional or social setting. Achieving this balance in self-confidence contributes to balanced emotional intelligence, enhancing your social management skills and leading to greater overall success.

To foster genuine personal growth and enhance self-esteem and confidence, it is essential to embrace the concept of accepting our mistakes. When we make an error, we must acknowledge that it is now in the past, and dwelling on it serves no purpose. Instead, the key is to focus on the valuable lessons gained from the experience. Embracing this mindset supports a growth-oriented outlook and nurtures emotional intelligence in a healthy manner.

By cultivating such an approach, we not only distance ourselves from having low emotional intelligence but also remain grounded and humble. This practice is a catalyst for profound personal development and has the potential to attract others to us. Once we master the art of accepting our faults, flaws, and mistakes, we can release the burden they carry and wholeheartedly trust in our ability to become the best version of ourselves.

Experiencing Anxiety

Anxiety can manifest in two ways, either as occasional anxiety or as permanent anxiety. The latter is the kind one would rather not have as it tends to persist unless intentionally treated. Occasional anxiety, on the other hand, is not constant and arises during times of stress or pressure to perform. It often accompanies the fear of failure, whether in the workplace, professional settings, or social environments. Experiencing occasional anxiety is a normal part of life that everyone encounters at some point or another.

Facing anxiety can make one feel helpless and overwhelmed, be it a temporary anxiety attack lasting a few hours or lingering for weeks. It is crucial to understand that anxiety is real, and denying its existence does not help. Acceptance of this emotional state can be challenging for many people, as nobody wants to admit that something might be wrong with them. However, acknowledging and addressing anxiety is essential for one's mental well-being.

Anxiety can be intense and, when it becomes a chronic condition, can lead to depression. Acceptance and recognition of anxiety are the first steps toward managing its symptoms effectively. While there may be hesitation in accepting the presence of an anxiety disorder, understanding it is key to finding ways to improve the experience.

Acknowledging that one may be dealing with an anxiety disorder does not require broadcasting it to the world. Instead, it offers an opportunity to understand oneself better and seek appropriate help. By accepting anxiety, one gains insight into their emotional struggles, enabling them to confront fears and work towards achieving a better quality of life.

Evaluate if you experience the following indications:

- Breathing rapidly (hyperventilating)
- Difficulty concentrating

- Experiencing sweating and trembling
- Feeling nervous, tense, weak, tired, or restless
- Sensing danger and panic
- Nightmares or difficulty sleeping
- Feeling the need to avoid situations that trigger anxiety
- Experiencing gastrointestinal problems
- Unable to control worrying
- Constantly concerned about things beyond your control

Anxiety disorders encompass various conditions:

- Agoraphobia: Fear and avoidance of places or situations that can lead to panic, helplessness, feeling trapped, or embarrassment.
- Generalized anxiety disorder: Persistent or excessive anxiety involving uncontrollable worry about events or activities, often accompanied by other anxiety disorders or depression.
- Panic disorder: Repeated episodes of sudden intense fear, terror, or anxiety leading to panic attacks, with symptoms like shortness of breath, palpitations, chest pain, and thoughts of impending doom. It can result in anxiety about these experiences or avoiding situations where they might occur.
- Medical anxiety: Intense panic or anxiety directly linked to physical health issues.
- Selective mutism: Consistent inability to speak in certain settings or situations, affecting children and sometimes adults, including school, social settings, and work, impacting their functioning in those environments.
- Social anxiety disorder: Fear and avoidance of social situations due to self-consciousness, embarrassment, or concerns about judgment, leading to extremely high levels of anxiety.
- Phobias: Intense anxiety triggered by a specific object or situation, leading to the avoidance of the phobic stimulus to prevent panic attacks.
- Childhood Separation Anxiety Disorder - A condition observed in children

during their developmental phase, triggered by the experience of being separated from their parents or guardians.

- Substance-Induced Anxiety Disorders - These disorders manifest with severe panic and anxiety symptoms resulting from the misuse of medication, drugs, or alcohol. Individuals with this disorder often feel dependent on these substances and fear being without them.
- Other Specified and Unspecified Anxiety Disorders - This category includes anxiety disorders or phobias that cause distress and disruption in an individual's life but do not fall under specific diagnostic criteria.

When it comes to seeking medical attention or diagnosing yourself:

If you find yourself constantly worried about a potential anxiety disorder or struggling with persistent feelings of helplessness and disruptive behavior, it is crucial to consider seeking medical treatment promptly. Pay attention to how anxiety affects different aspects of your life, including work, relationships, and overall well-being. Seeking help is essential if you are experiencing chronic fear, depression, uncontrollable anxiety, substance abuse issues, or if you suspect that your anxiety might be related to underlying medical conditions.

On the other hand, if you believe that your anxiety is temporary and might resolve on its own without worsening over time, you may not require immediate professional assistance. Experiencing occasional stress and panic is a normal part of life. However, if your anxiety becomes more persistent or severe, it is crucial to take it seriously and address it with appropriate support.

Medical professionals recommend the following top treatment options for anxiety disorders:

1. Antidepressant medications: These prescribed medications are often used in combination with Cognitive Behavioral Therapy (CBT) to address both anxiety and depression. Antidepressants typically contain selective

serotonin reuptake inhibitors (SSRIs) to minimize side effects compared to older medications like beta-blockers.

2. Cognitive Behavioral Therapy (CBT): This therapeutic approach is employed alongside antidepressant medications to treat anxiety, depression, and fear. CBT helps patients learn how to regain control over their emotions and lives.

3. Exercise: An effective and straightforward solution for releasing positive hormones like serotonin in the brain. Engaging in regular exercise benefits both mental and physical well-being, providing a sense of control and accomplishment, which contributes to overall relaxation and well-being.

4. Relaxation methods: To counter feelings of being overwhelmed by anxiety and depression, incorporating relaxation techniques can be highly beneficial. These methods include meditation, mindfulness practices, engaging in relaxing hobbies like reading or yoga, deep breathing exercises, and listening to calming music. They help relax the nervous system and improve daily life quality.

To prevent the onset of anxiety disorders, it is crucial to seek early help as it is a mental health condition that necessitates treatment. Delaying treatment can make it more challenging to manage the disorder as it may worsen over time. Avoiding alcohol, drugs, and cigarette smoking can help prevent the exacerbation of anxiety. If the condition is in its early stages, staying active, participating in social interactions, and nurturing supportive relationships are recommended strategies.

The Presence of Anxiety in Relationships

Picture a scenario where you react excessively to stress, going to great lengths to over-prepare for even the simplest of social events or a minor storm. At first glance, this might appear harmless, as being over-prepared seems better than being underprepared, right?

While that may be true, this behavior could indicate the presence of an anxiety disorder. When you find yourself having anxious thoughts about things that others consider simple, it's possible that you are dealing with anxiety. Although it might seem like an underlying issue to you, it can be draining for your partner or anyone else in your life. Overestimating and dwelling on potential negative outcomes isn't something everyone wants to hear about, and this could have a negative impact on your relationships.

Now imagine if this overreacting extends to situations at work, where you stress excessively over responsibilities, deadlines, and other work-related matters. This could lead to bringing a lot of stress and anxiety home, impacting your family and making it difficult for you to relax. A tense relationship is far from pleasant.

Anxiety can manifest in various ways, from being easily startled to experiencing difficulty concentrating, sleeping problems, overthinking, headaches, muscle tension, sweating, trembling, and nausea. These symptoms not only affect your physical and mental health but also disrupt the lives of those around you.

If you've ever thought that anxiety is something you can simply brush off or hide from others, think again. It has a profound effect on various aspects of your life and can damage relationships, breaking down trust and causing you to miss out on opportunities. Anxiety can even hinder your career and social interactions, pulling you away from the present and leading to excessive procrastination.

Seeking professional help is crucial, as addressing anxiety can lead to a healthier and more fulfilling life, allowing you to rebuild trust and maintain better relationships. Putting aside pride and acknowledging the negative impact of anxiety should be reason enough to take action and regain control over your life while nurturing the relationships that matter to you.

Social Anxiety

Social anxiety is an anxiety disorder characterized by an intense fear of being observed and judged by others. For those who haven't experienced it, this fear may seem unimaginable. How can one be afraid of people? Can it be overcome, and what makes it so distressing that it leads to panic attacks without improvement?

Social anxiety is often misunderstood. The idea of entering a room full of people or facing a crowd can be overwhelming and limiting. People with social anxiety don't choose to have this trait. While it may never be completely cured, with practice, one can learn to manage it better. Unfortunately, society tends to judge individuals with social anxiety, labeling them as shy, introverted, or even "weird."

Being different isn't inherently negative, as uniqueness can lead to success. However, when social anxiety limits one's ability to function normally, it becomes problematic. People with social anxiety often don't even recognize it as a disorder, attributing it to shyness or social awkwardness. Nonetheless, they wish they could be rid of it because it hinders them from engaging in regular activities that others take for granted, such as meeting new people, speaking in public, or enjoying social events.

People with social anxiety may struggle with various situations, including making eye contact, dating, eating in front of others, attending school or work, and initiating conversations. These constraints arise from a fear of judgment, offending others, humiliation, or embarrassment. Past traumatic experiences, such as bullying or low self-esteem, can also contribute to the development of social anxiety.

Social anxiety affects each individual uniquely, leading to different responses to stress. As it can hinder a healthy life and the formation of meaningful relationships, it is crucial to address it in any way possible.

Surprisingly, there is a way to deal with social anxiety, even though it may seem insurmountable. Despite the desire to make friends and engage socially, those experiencing social anxiety often hold back due to fear and difficulty communicating in social settings. It is not a voluntary choice; rather, it is an innate response. To change this, individuals must confront their fears and anxieties. Joining a support group with others facing similar challenges can be the answer for those yearning to be sociable and open to those around them.

Besides the observable symptoms, social anxiety can trigger emotional responses such as nervousness, negative emotional cycles, blushing, a racing heartbeat, dry mouth, sweating, and muscle twitches. When triggered, individuals may experience intense anxiety and develop body dysmorphia, feeling extremely self-conscious. Although they may be aware of the irrationality of their feelings, the fears persist and become chronic. Cognitive Behavioral Therapy (CBT), as mentioned earlier, is an excellent solution for addressing social anxiety. It can modify the neural pathways in the brain, offering hope for those struggling with daily constraints and feelings.

The first step towards recovery is seeking help and a proper diagnosis from a specialist experienced in treating the disorder. CBT, combined with active behavioral therapy in a group setting, helps patients work through real-life challenges with support from fellow group members. Over time, individuals learn to approach and handle social anxiety with ease. With the right therapy, support, patience, and hard work, social anxiety can become a treatable condition. CBT effectively transforms thoughts, emotions, and behaviors toward people and social situations. By being compliant and dedicated to overcoming the disorder, success in recovery is achievable.

Conquering the Dread of Panic Attacks

Panic attacks arise from sudden bursts of anxiety that overwhelm both the body and mind. These episodes typically last for about 10 minutes and are often terrifying and dreaded. Many individuals who experience panic attacks are apprehensive about resuming their normal lives and tend to avoid social interactions and settings, fearing the loss of control. Dealing with panic attacks can take an emotional toll, but with the development of effective coping skills, managing the symptoms becomes more feasible.

Panic attacks can occur at any moment and encompass a mix of uncomfortable physical sensations, distressing thoughts, and heightened emotions. Physical symptoms like sweating, shaking, and shortness of breath can exacerbate and trigger fearful ideas and intense anxiety-related feelings. These unpleasant sensations significantly impact mental health. People undergoing panic attacks may even mistake the experience for a heart attack or feel as though they are losing their sanity. Panic attacks can be triggered by various anxieties, and their effects can persist for hours beyond the actual 10-minute episode.

To overcome anxiety, it is essential to confront and overcome the fears that contribute to panic attacks. By facing things that seem scary or intimidating, one can reduce the fear associated with them. Although it may be challenging to feel in control or avoid feeling judged during panic attacks, it is crucial to remind oneself that one is capable of halting these episodes and regain a sense of control.

Achieving this can be accomplished by following these steps:

1. Educate yourself. By gaining a comprehensive understanding of what contributes not only to your panic attacks but also to your mental relationship with the fear of panic attacks, you will gain clarity about your symptoms. This knowledge will help you realize that there is nothing physically wrong with you and that you have the ability to overcome the notion that there is. The more informed you become about the triggers and underlying causes, the less fearful you will be of your symptoms, increasing your chances of moving past them.

2. Embrace and modify your response to panic attacks. Once you have developed a clear understanding of the symptoms you experience, the

next step is to acknowledge and accept the source of your panic attacks. Although this may not be an easy task, accepting it can lead to better recovery. Reflect on your past experiences, acknowledge your fearful feelings, and recognize the anxiety and nervousness you experience during your symptoms. Shifting your perception of panic attacks will make it much easier to cope with them effectively. Instead of merely reacting to panic attacks, you can now choose to deal with them constructively. Additionally, try practicing relaxation techniques each time you feel a panic attack coming on. This may include deep breathing exercises, yoga, or engaging in mindfulness practices. Changing how you respond to panic attacks will empower you to gain control over them with practice.

To sum it up, here are the essential steps you should take:

1. Acknowledge: Recognize your episodes or feelings and the symptoms of increased anxiety, and take a moment to understand what is happening to you.
2. Accept it: Instead of resisting your symptoms, embrace the fact that you are having a panic attack and decide not to give it power over you.
3. Respond intentionally: Rather than letting your mind run wild, deliberately choose an alternative response. Take a moment to consider your reaction before you act, and shift your perspective on what is happening. Approach the situation mindfully and remember that you have control over the few minutes it occurs.

The Art of Influencing People

Taking inspiration from these words and gaining self-perspective while not caring excessively about what others think of you is indeed a positive attitude. However, there are certain individuals whose opinions you should consider to maintain equal respect in your relationships. These may include your boss, co-workers, family, and close friends. Though not everyone aspires to be an influencer, the truth is that we all have an impact on people, whether we are aware of it or not.

Becoming an intentional influencer is an art that requires effort. You need to learn how to analyze and understand people. For instance, in a business context, when dealing with customers or potential clients, being able to read them is crucial to approaching them in a way that benefits you or your company. Effective communication and negotiation skills are vital in sales and marketing, as experts in these fields understand how to capture people's attention and achieve their goals.

Similar to a skilled sales or marketing consultant, you too can learn how to convince and influence people. With practice, you can approach individuals and articulate your thoughts effectively during meetings. Influencing others is not just limited to improving work outcomes; it can also be valuable in forging new connections and enhancing existing relationships. When you master the skill of influencing people, you can use it for positive purposes, making a positive impact on the lives of those around you. This, in turn, earns you more respect and, if you are in a leadership position, establishes you as an authoritative figure.

There are several effective steps you can take to positively influence people:

Step 1: Prioritize giving people what they want. To successfully influence others, it's essential to focus on meeting their desires instead of solely pursuing your own agenda. By catering to their needs and wishes, you demonstrate respect and build trust in your relationships. Being selfless and considering others' preferences makes you more likable and fosters a positive connection. While you don't have to always do exactly what others want, incorporating a reasonable amount of accommodation into your interactions can significantly improve your influence on them. If you tend to be self-centered, adopting this approach may be challenging, but if not, it will come naturally.

Here are some simple tips to help you achieve this:

- Acknowledge and learn from your own mistakes and frustrations.
- Observe and gain insights from the mistakes of others.
- Communicate more efficiently by being direct and straightforward in your speech.
- Introduce positive elements like motivation and uplifting experiences to create opportunities for growth.
- Surround yourself with successful individuals, as they can shape your reality.
- Shift your focus onto others to gain their respect, without attempting to convince them. Instead, find out how you can contribute positively to their lives.

Step 2: Highlight the significance of the people you interact with. Recognize the importance of the individuals you deal with, both in your personal and professional life. When you hold a position of leadership or management, valuing your employees or team members will have a profound impact on their responses. When people feel valued and appreciated, they go beyond meeting minimum expectations in their work. Appreciation fosters an environment where work becomes enjoyable and fulfilling, rather than merely a task to maintain employment. Demonstrating that others are important creates a sense of respect and trust, encouraging them to reciprocate and contribute more to your relationship. This principle applies not only in professional settings but also in personal interactions, where treating others with significance leads to mutual respect and deeper connections.

Step 3: Foster emotional connections and empowerment. To successfully influence others, the first step is establishing emotional connections with them. When you connect on an emotional level, there's no need to seek help or feel guilty about it. This connection leads to a better understanding between you and the other person, which becomes a powerful tool for influencing them, particularly in a leadership role. By emotionally connecting with others, you gain insights into their needs and perspectives, enabling you to influence them more effectively. In a business setting, forming these connections with employees helps create a harmonious workflow and builds trust between you and potential business partners. Each person in business has unique thinking, so dealing with a diverse range of individuals allows you to learn and adapt your approach successfully.

Step 4: Embrace and respect diverse opinions. Always value and respect the opinions of others. Refrain from declaring someone's opinions as wrong, but instead, view failures as opportunities to learn. By showing respect for others' viewpoints, the focus shifts away from you, allowing for open and constructive discussions. When someone approaches you with a differing opinion, consider their perspective thoughtfully and respond by expressing respect for their viewpoint while offering your alternative perspective. This approach, which respects others' self-esteem, allows you to influence people positively with your ideas and perspectives.

Step 5: Lead, don't boss. Recognize the crucial difference between being a leader and a boss. A true leader is approachable, collaborates with others on projects and ideas, and respects their visions and goals. They actively support their team, push them in the right direction, and invest time in fostering growth and development. On the other hand, a boss merely issues orders, shirks responsibilities onto others, and focuses on self-centered priorities. They fail to invest time in their team and may take advantage of their subordinates' efforts. If your goal is to influence others in a leadership position, be a good leader rather than a boss. Effective leadership hinges on communication and understanding, especially with those who work for you.

By adopting this approach, you maintain the respect of your co-workers and business relations, making you a successful and influential leader.

Step 6: Show empathy and constructive feedback. When individuals make mistakes, approach the situation with empathy and a positive attitude toward learning from those errors. It is crucial not to scold or excessively focus on their mistakes. Instead, adopt a sympathetic approach, providing professional and helpful feedback that encourages them to learn and improve. To influence others effectively, offer constructive guidance, suggesting ways they can enhance their performance or learn from the mistakes they made. You may even challenge them to approach the project or task from a different angle, allowing them the opportunity to learn, grow, and build trust. By adopting this approach, they will feel more comfortable seeking your guidance and will be motivated to persevere and keep trying until they achieve success instead of accepting failure. This approach instills confidence in their abilities and fosters a sense of pride in their work. By employing this strategy, you can influence others to become better versions of themselves, improve their skills, and foster personal growth.

Mastering the Skill of Effective People Analysis

To exert influence over others, it is essential to possess the ability to deeply understand who they are. Without a clear understanding of individuals, comprehending their needs becomes challenging. The art of analyzing people empowers you to gather crucial information, enabling you to make a significant impact on them or even establish better connections. To analyze people effectively, you must be adept at interpreting both their verbal and nonverbal cues. While not everyone may be straightforward, with the right knowledge and sufficient practice, you can still gain valuable insights into people's thoughts and emotions.

An inability to pick up on social cues can hinder your understanding of others' feelings and requirements, leading to difficulties in building positive relationships. To genuinely influence others, it is imperative to demonstrate vulnerability and embrace various forms of information. This requires letting go of preconceptions, emotional baggage, resentments, ego, and negative past experiences. By maintaining objectivity and refraining from judging others, you open yourself up to receiving information and insights that can aid in understanding them better. This mindset allows you to focus on the goal of learning more about others rather than being burdened by personal biases that might hinder a comprehensive analysis.

The capacity to read people applies to all areas of life, whether it's your boss, coworker, spouse, friend, or even a stranger. Analyzing people entails paying attention to details and accumulating sufficient information to interact with them effectively and make a positive impact. By honing this skill, you can enhance your interpersonal relationships and wield a positive influence on those around you.

When analyzing someone, you engage in reading and understanding them, which involves the following steps:

1.Observe Body Language.

Did you know that our spoken words only account for a mere 7%, sometimes even less, of our overall communication? Surprisingly, body language plays a much more significant role, accounting for 55% of how we convey our messages. Even the tone of our voice holds more influence, contributing 30% to how others perceive us. This realization validates the well-known saying: "It's not what you say, but how you say it." This valuable insight doesn't just come from a wise man, Professor Albert Mehrabian, but stands as a practical truth.

With this understanding, it's important not to judge people solely based on their spoken words. Instead, one should pay close attention to their tone, actions, appearance, and overall body language when communicating. Rather than becoming overly intense or excessively analytical, it is best to stay relaxed and consider all these elements.

Take note of someone's appearance and how they present themselves through their clothing choices. Their posture is another telling aspect; a confident individual often holds their head high, while someone with a different stance might be conveying various emotions like shyness, surprise, loneliness, sadness, stress, embarrassment, or a lack of self-confidence.

Even the way people move provides valuable insights. The way they lean, cross their arms or legs, fidget, bite their lip or nails, and touch their hair or face can reveal a lot about their demeanor and state of mind. The face, especially, is highly expressive. In the moment, facial expressions provide glimpses of thoughts and feelings, while long-term emotions can leave their mark, such as frown lines indicating concern or overthinking, crow's feet showing joy over time, pursed lips suggesting bitterness, anger, or contempt, and a clenched jaw or teeth signifying tension. By attentively observing body language, we can gain valuable insights into a person's thoughts, emotions, and character.

2. Rely On Your Instincts.

Beyond verbal communication and body language, understanding others and being understood also involves considering intuition. Intuition is that gut feeling that informs you whether someone is trustworthy or not. While some individuals possess strong intuition, others might not rely on it as much. Intuition provides nonverbal insights that emerge when you observe someone closely or when you grasp something about them beyond what is evident on the surface. It enables you to perceive beyond the physical appearance and select better intuitive cues. To do this effectively, follow these steps:

- Listen to your gut, especially when you encounter someone for the first time. It captures the information and feelings you gather before your conscious mind starts forming judgments. Gut feelings can arise within seconds or minutes of meeting someone, offering clues about whether you can trust them or not.

- Pay attention to goosebumps. Although it might seem peculiar, goosebumps serve as signals from our intuition when we connect with something deeply, including people. Whether we are moved, inspired, or even scared, we may experience goosebumps. They can also occur during moments of déjà vu or when we encounter familiar situations or things.
- Be receptive to intuitive empathy. Empathy is a capacity shared by everyone, but its intensity varies. Some people possess high levels of empathy, allowing them to sense the emotions of others even without verbal communication. On the other hand, some individuals have less developed empathy. Empathy enables you to read people and understand their emotions. Cultivating a sense of selflessness and awareness of your surroundings can enhance your empathetic abilities. With greater empathy, you will find it easier to connect with others, build trust, and perceive people more accurately compared to those lacking in empathy.
- Rely on your instincts. Beyond verbal communication and body language, understanding others and being understood also involves considering intuition. Intuition is that gut feeling that informs you whether someone is trustworthy or not. While some individuals possess strong intuition, others might not rely on it as much. Intuition provides nonverbal insights that emerge when you observe someone closely or when you grasp something about them beyond what is evident on the surface. It enables you to perceive beyond the physical appearance and select better intuitive cues. To do this effectively, follow these steps:
- Listen to your gut, especially when you encounter someone for the first time. It captures the information and feelings you gather before your conscious mind starts forming judgments. Gut feelings can arise within seconds or minutes of meeting someone, offering clues about whether you can trust them or not.
- Pay attention to goosebumps. Although it might seem peculiar, goosebumps serve as signals from our intuition when we connect with something deeply, including people. Whether we are moved, inspired, or even scared, we may experience goosebumps. They can also occur during moments of déjà vu or when we encounter familiar situations or things.

- Be receptive to intuitive empathy. Empathy is a capacity shared by everyone, but its intensity varies. Some people possess high levels of empathy, allowing them to sense the emotions of others even without verbal communication. On the other hand, some individuals have less developed empathy. Empathy enables you to read people and understand their emotions. Cultivating a sense of selflessness and awareness of your surroundings can enhance your empathetic abilities. With greater empathy, you will find it easier to connect with others, build trust, and perceive people more accurately compared to those lacking in empathy.

3.Perceive Emotional Energy.

Emotions serve as expressions of our energy, whether we choose to display them overtly or not. They manifest through facial expressions and behavior, providing cues about people's disposition. When encountering others, you can sense whether they emit positive or negative energy, influencing your desire to engage with them.

To effectively read people's emotional energy, consider these strategies:

- Sense their presence: Pay attention to people's overall demeanor to discern their willingness to participate in conversations or be present in a particular setting. Emotions create an atmosphere that conveys valuable insights, helping you avoid misconceptions about them.
- Observe their eyes: Eyes reveal more than you might imagine. By attentively observing someone's eyes, you can decipher emotions such as anger, happiness, fear, or sadness. Additionally, eye contact can provide cues about their openness to intimacy or willingness to share thoughts and feelings.
- Listen to their voice and laugh tone: The volume and tone of people's voices convey significant information about their emotional state. By taking these aspects into account, you can better understand them and respond appropriately.
- Be aware of physical touch: Intuition can guide you in recognizing

emotional energy through physical contact. Pay attention to how it feels when someone shakes your hand or hugs you, as these gestures can reveal emotions such as trust, warmth, anxiety, or comfort.

By being attuned to these emotional cues, you can develop a deeper understanding of others and respond in ways that foster meaningful connections and communication.

Mastering Body Language Reading: 7 Expert Techniques

1.Analyzing Eye Behavior

As mentioned earlier, our eyes serve a greater purpose than just vision. People convey a lot through their eyes, especially those who are less talkative. Surprisingly, many individuals who refrain from excessive talking often feel misunderstood. They place higher value on body language than on verbal communication, despite still facing misunderstandings.

When considering the vast amount of communication conveyed through our bodies, particularly our eyes, the act of not speaking verbally suddenly appears more normal than using our voices. Our eyes can provide profound insights into someone's character, including cues like blink frequency and pupil dilation. When interacting with others, pay attention to their eyes, whether they maintain direct eye contact or look away. Also, observe how frequently they avert their gaze.

Looking away while speaking may indicate deception, disinterest, or boredom. Conversely, looking downwards could imply nervousness or submissiveness. Moreover, pupils dilate when cognitive effort increases, so dilated pupils can signify genuine intentions, such as liking someone.

However, detecting pupil dilation may be challenging, particularly with darker eye colors. Be cautious when intensely staring into someone's eyes to avoid sending misleading signals about your own feelings.

By studying people's eyes, you can also identify signs of stress, often seen through increased blinking. The rate of blinking can reveal whether someone is relaxed or tense. Rapid blinking, accompanied by touching the mouth or face, might indicate deception.

Additionally, glancing at someone without turning their face may signal a desire to get your attention or initiate a conversation. Meanwhile, looking upwards and to the right during a conversation can imply lying, while looking upwards and to the left suggests truthfulness. Such distinctions can be understood as people looking to the right use their imagination to tell stories, while looking up and to the left indicates recalling memories.

2.Observe Proximity and Connection.

The distance between individuals when they sit or stand can reveal the nature of their relationship. You will naturally be closer to your spouse, friend, or family member than you would be to a mere acquaintance or stranger. Proximity serves as a reliable indicator of trust and comfort between two people. When someone moves closer to you or pulls away, it signifies the level of trust and connection they feel. However, cultural norms can influence the preferred distance, making proximity less reliable in those cases. Still, in most instances, it can provide valuable insights into how at ease individuals are with each other.

3.Decode Facial Expressions.

Touch and Smile. Facial expressions are a key element of nonverbal behavior, and they often reveal true emotions. To understand others better, pay close attention to their facial cues, as people are usually less guarded in expressing themselves this way. A smile, especially when genuine, is a powerful expression of friendliness and can quickly earn someone's trust. A genuine smile also reflects a happy and positive personality. On the other hand, a fake smile may indicate disapproval, sadness, irritation, or negative emotions. A half-smile can suggest sarcasm or uncertainty.

It's essential to consider the context when interpreting facial expressions. Observe if there were signs of displeasure before someone smiled, such as a frown or pursed lips, as this can provide a better understanding of their emotions.

Additionally, watch for any touching of the mouth while someone is speaking, as it can indicate potential deception, regardless of the type of smile they display. By observing the mouth, you can gain insights into a person's emotions and level of comfort in your presence.

4.Observe Head Movements.

Pay attention to how people nod their heads during conversations, as it holds significance similar to the pace of their speech. A slow nod indicates genuine interest in what you are saying, while a faster nod suggests a desire for you to conclude your speech quickly. When someone tilts their head to the side, it shows interest in the other person's perspective. On the other hand, tilting the head backward may indicate uncertainty or suspicion. Directing one's head towards another person's face signals a strong connection between them.

5.Analyze Hand and Feet Gestures.

Although feet might seem inconspicuous, they, along with hands, are crucial nonverbal cues to observe when reading body language. The positioning of hands, such as placing them in pockets or making unintentional gestures, can convey nervousness, deception, or truthfulness. Paying attention to someone's hands can reveal their thoughts and intentions.

Supporting the head with a hand, resting the elbow on a table, signifies attentive listening and focus. Conversely, resting both elbows on the table may indicate boredom. Holding an object between oneself and others acts as a nonverbal barrier and suggests intentional avoidance of communication.

Feet can be a powerful source of body language that is often overlooked. People naturally point their feet in the direction they want to go, revealing their interest or lack thereof in a conversation. By observing someone's feet, you can gauge their level of engagement and determine if they are eager to leave the conversation. Likewise, if you want to appear engaged, make an effort to point your feet towards the person you are speaking with.

6. Take Note of Mirroring Behavior.

Mirroring, in terms of body language, involves mimicking the gestures and postures of the person you are communicating with. For instance, if they have their hands folded, you might also adopt a similar gesture to establish a better connection with them. Mirroring fosters improved interaction between individuals. Moreover, observe whether the other person starts mirroring you during the conversation. If they do, it indicates their comfort level while talking to you, which is a positive sign. By occasionally adjusting your own body posture, you can gauge their level of engagement and commitment to the conversation. Utilizing mirroring strategically can even encourage others to become more involved, as people naturally tend to notice and respond to how you sit, stand, walk, or interact.

7.Pay Attention to Arm Movements.

A person's arms can be seen as a gateway to their feelings and thoughts. When someone crosses their arms while conversing with you or others, it may come across as a defensive or blocking gesture. It's essential to avoid displaying a closed or unwelcoming demeanor when communicating with someone. opt for an open posture instead to convey confidence and ease. Folded arms might suggest feelings of anxiety, closed-mindedness, or vulnerability, none of which you want to convey during a conversation. The same applies to the person you are engaging with. By consciously adjusting your overall body posture, you can exude confidence and present yourself as an effective communicator. It's fascinating how much meaning arm movements can convey, isn't it?

Chapter Dark Psychology

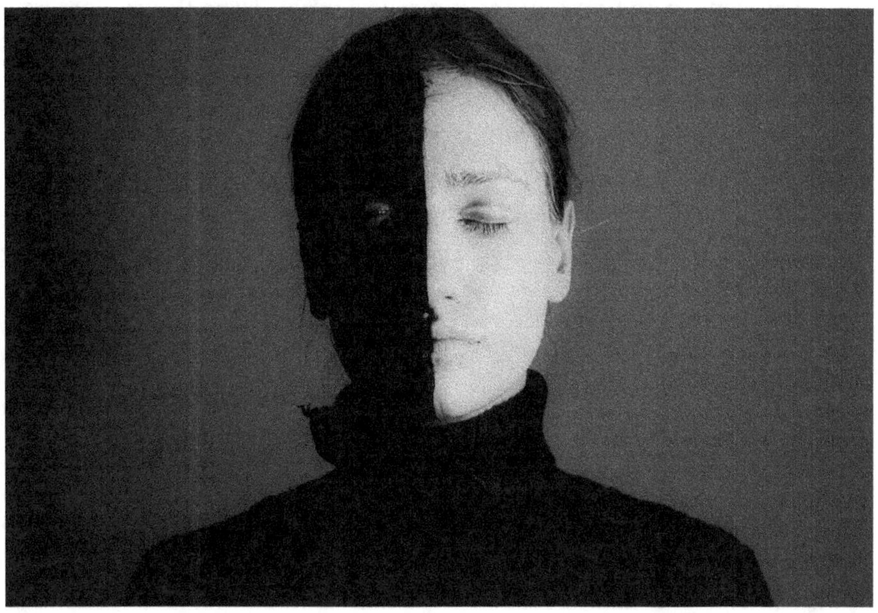

Dark psychology is closely associated with manipulation, encompassing the science of manipulation and mind control, which should be avoided. Learning to read body language, understanding social cues, and improving our ability to comprehend others are all beneficial skills for effective communication. However, when the focus shifts from empathizing and genuinely connecting with others to manipulating them for personal gain, it becomes problematic. Manipulative behavior can cause harm to others and lead one to believe such actions are normal, leading to a dangerous pattern of repetition.

Dark psychology is a lesser-known aspect of psychology compared to the more positive branches. Many people may not even be aware of its existence, yet individuals who employ dark psychology tactics can be found among us daily. If psychology revolves around studying human behavior and interactions, what does the dark side entail?

This phenomenon relies on manipulation, coercion, and persuasion for selfish reasons or to harm others in various ways. "The Dark Triad" is a term often used in the context of dark psychology, effectively describing its characteristics. Criminologists and psychologists often refer to the Dark Psychology Triad to analyze criminal behavior or any behavior that appears dangerous or problematic.

The Dark Triad encompasses three traits:

- Narcissism, characterized by egotism, lack of empathy, and being demanding.
- Machiavellianism, involving the use of manipulative techniques to deceive and exploit others, often accompanied by a lack of morality.
- Psychopathy, displaying a charming and friendly demeanor while also exhibiting traits of selfishness, impulsivity, lack of empathy, and remorselessness.

Some individuals may believe they have no control over the people they associate with, but as adults, they typically have full control over this aspect of their lives. While there might be unique situations where it is challenging to distance oneself from people with Dark Triad traits, unless it poses a danger, efforts should be made to remove toxic individuals from one's life.

The traits associated with the Dark Triad can also manifest temporarily in children's behavior, especially in teenagers, as they experiment with different approaches to achieve their desires. Teenagers, and even loved ones, may display behaviors such as lying, withdrawal, restricting choices, love flooding, denial, semantic manipulation, and reverse psychology.

Dark psychology is commonly practiced by various individuals, including:

- Narcissists: People who exude a sense of self-importance and seek adoration or worship. Diagnosing narcissistic traits requires professional evaluation, and they can be dangerous, manipulative, and unethical in maintaining trust with others.
- Politicians: Surprisingly, politicians can employ dark psychological tactics to achieve their goals, even if it involves making decisions with little remorse about the consequences for the population.
- Attorneys: Lawyers, too, often resort to dark psychological tactics to win cases and obtain desired outcomes.
- Sociopaths: Like narcissists, sociopathic individuals require clinical diagnosis. They can be charming and intelligent but lack emotionality and remorse, leading them to use dark tactics to exploit friends and family.
- Leaders and public speakers: Even high-ranking individuals, such as managers and monarchs, may utilize dark psychological traits to gain advantages, increase compliance, and improve performance from those they oversee.
- Salespeople: Motivated salespeople may resort to manipulation and lying to achieve their objectives, using various dark psychological techniques to boost sales by exaggerating product benefits.
- Selfish individuals: Anyone with a selfish agenda can display dark psychological tendencies, regardless of their profession.

It is essential to recognize these behaviors and be cautious of their potential negative impacts on society and personal relationships.

Evaluating dark psychology is possible, whether you're concerned about your own behavior or that of someone you know. To assess the intentions and motivations behind your actions, ask yourself the following questions:

- Am I completely open and honest?
- What is the purpose of this interaction? Who benefits from it, and how?
- How do I feel about my approach in specific interactions?
- Will this interaction benefit the other person in the long run?
- Will my or their tactics contribute to building trust in relevant relationships?

By honestly considering the answers to these questions, you can determine whether you are engaging in unjustifiable behavior related to dark psychology. While it may be tempting to resort to such tactics to achieve success in relationships, work, leadership, or other aspects of life, it can lead to consuming and damaging consequences. Instead, choosing to do things right can lead to long-term influence, credibility, and positive relationships with others. Building and maintaining a good reputation can be challenging, but it is worth the effort to avoid the pitfalls of dark psychology, which can result in broken relationships, a negative character, and long-term failure. Prioritizing ethical behavior and doing the right thing is ultimately more rewarding and beneficial in the long run.

Exploring Narcissism

As a significant component of the Dark Triad, narcissism is a trait that can be found in various individuals. Some people are completely consumed by it, while others show only subtle signs. It's likely that everyone has encountered someone with narcissistic tendencies in their life. Narcissistic Personality Disorder (NPD) is characterized by an inflated self-opinion and a constant desire for attention. Those with NPD often exhibit selfishness and may feel unhappy or disappointed when they don't receive the praise or admiration, they believe they deserve. They are often seen as conceited, vain, or snobbish, and despite their initial charm, they become challenging to be around once their true colors are revealed. NPD can lead to difficulties in school, relationships, and career, but with lifestyle changes and therapy, it can be effectively managed.

Individuals with NPD often face challenging responses from others due to their arrogance, demanding nature, and tendency to exaggerate their talents and accomplishments. They are preoccupied with beauty, success, and power, and may engage in impulsive behaviors, including addictive habits like alcohol, drugs, smoking, or gambling, which they need to gain control of to recover from their disorder.

The causes of NPD can often be traced back to childhood neglect, abuse, trauma, or excessive parental love and pampering. Cultural influences, unrealistic expectations imposed on children, and sexual promiscuity can also contribute to the development of NPD. Understanding these underlying factors is crucial for effectively addressing and managing narcissistic tendencies.

While this disorder may initially seem challenging to address, it is treatable through psychotherapy. If NPD co-occurs with depression, anxiety, or any other mental health condition, individuals with NPD may need to use medications alongside talk therapy for effective treatment. Psychotherapy plays a crucial role in helping those with NPD develop more positive inter-actions, leading to substantial improvements in their personal relationships and providing them with a fresh perspective and a better understanding of themselves. Moreover, it can aid in cultivating healthier and more sustainable emotions. Additionally, psychotherapy assists individuals with NPD in enhancing their relationships with colleagues, acknowledging their strengths, and building resilience to handle criticism, failures, and self-esteem issues, while also setting realistic goals.

Living with NPD, individuals must recognize that they have control over their behavior and can change it whenever they desire. While altering and managing narcissistic traits may require effort, the process of treatment can significantly transform and enhance their lives.

When Should You Consider Psychotherapy?

Psychotherapy is a form of therapy employed by psychologists to assist individuals in addressing mental health issues. However, there are numerous reasons why people may seek or be recommended for psychotherapy, ranging from feeling overwhelmed to struggling with minor problems. If you find yourself feeling overwhelmed or misunderstood, it's important to understand that you are not alone. There are effective ways to address the challenges that may be affecting your life. Emotional and mental well-being deserve greater attention, considering that over a quarter of American adults' experience anxiety, depression, or some form of mental disorder within a single year. It is essential for both children and adults to recognize that it's okay to experience anxiety, stress, depression, or feelings of being different. Support is available to help them feel better, and seeking help is not a sign of weakness but an act of courage, strength, and the desire to improve one's life. Seeking help should be seen as a positive step towards personal growth and well-being (American Psychological Association, n.d.).

There are various factors that can contribute to emotional and mental health challenges, such as relationship issues, stress, substance abuse, addiction, job loss or conflict, the death of a loved one, trauma, and many others. All these issues can benefit from therapy and psychotherapy can be instrumental in achieving a happier, healthier, and more fulfilling life. It can also enhance productivity in school or work and inspire individuals to surpass their own expectations.

Psychotherapy encompasses different approaches, including interpersonal therapy and cognitive-behavioral therapy (CBT), among others, which provide effective ways to work through problems. This collaborative treatment involves working with a psychologist specialized in the relevant field to address your specific needs. In therapy, the psychologist offers a safe and supportive space where you can freely discuss any topic. Their nonjudgmental and objective approach allows you to talk about things that may be difficult to share with others.

During therapy sessions, you and the psychologist work together to identify and modify thoughts, feelings, and behavior patterns that may hinder your well-being. Through the process, you'll acquire new skills to cope with present and future challenges, making your journey towards personal growth more effective.

Psychotherapy becomes essential when you are feeling overwhelmed, sad, isolated, or hopeless. If your efforts and the support from your family and friends do not lead to improvements, seeking the help of a psychologist is recommended. Difficulties in communication, concentration, excessive worrying, anxiety, tension, and stress, which may lead to harmful behaviors, also indicate the need for assistance. Regardless of the nature of the issues you are facing, there are psychotherapists specializing in various areas who can provide suitable treatment. During your initial appointment, you will be assessed, and then directed to a psychologist specializing in addressing your specific needs. You will receive a personalized treatment plan, which may or may not involve medication, along with ongoing therapy sessions with the psychologist.

Neuro-Linguistic Programming

Neuro-Linguistic Programming (NLP) involves studying successful individuals who have achieved their goals and developed strong characters, actively working towards success rather than merely discussing or thinking about it. Merely talking or thinking about goals often leads to limited progress. To enhance your effectiveness in all aspects of life, especially in pursuing your goals, learning about NLP can be valuable. NLP focuses on language, thoughts, ideas, and behavior patterns, utilizing diverse experiences and outcomes.

In the NLP approach, all human actions are considered positive, even when plans fail, as they provide valuable learning experiences. The concept originated in California in 1970 through the collaboration of Richard Bandler, an information scientist, and John Grinder, a linguist. They wrote books on NLP, based on techniques to identify language patterns and support cognitive processes. Today, NLP is globally utilized in various fields such as medicine, law, counseling, business, sports, military, education, and performing arts.

NLP effectively employs three main elements: action, modeling, and effective communication. By understanding how someone achieves a goal or task, one can replicate and share the process with others. NLP's decades-long implementation makes it a reliable practice to achieve goals effectively. Implementing NLP allows you to gain insights into your own and others' perspectives, providing a clearer vision of personal desires and facilitating faster progress towards them. Understanding others' perspectives enhances communication and fosters healthy relationships, while continuous learning about various perspectives enriches your interactions throughout life.

NLP is an experiential approach that emphasizes the importance of performing similar actions to fully understand a person's words or behaviors. Practitioners of NLP believe in the power of communication, learning, and personal growth. The NLP framework includes six logical levels, each interconnected and influencing one another when undergoing changes:

1. Purpose - Involving spirituality and connection to something bigger, such as ethics or religion, representing the highest level of change.
2. Beliefs and values - Encompassing one's belief system, principles, and what holds significance.
3. Personal identity - How individuals perceive themselves, including roles and responsibilities.
4. Capabilities - Focusing on skills and expertise, especially in professional aspects.

5. Behaviors - Specific actions performed daily, representing how individuals present themselves to others.
6. Environment - The settings where one lives, operates, and interacts with others, representing the lowest level of change.

NLP is taught in therapy and emphasizes the differences between reality and individual beliefs, recognizing that everyone's perception of the world is unique. NLP therapists understand how patients think and operate within their limiting or unique perspectives. Practitioners of NLP learn to access different representational systems through cues like eye movements and gestures.

Therapists work with aspiring practitioners to understand their thought processes, emotions, aspirations, and behavioral patterns, helping them discover and strengthen beneficial skills while replacing unproductive ones. This approach produces sustainable results, enhancing cognitive and behavioral patterns, improving communication between conscious and unconscious processes, enhancing problem-solving abilities, and boosting creativity. NLP is effective in treating various conditions, including anxiety, phobias, depression, communication issues, addiction, and more.

While NLP is regarded as an effective treatment option, its complexity and lack of empirical evidence supporting treatment claims make it challenging to comprehend fully. However, countless testimonials from people who have experienced NLP treatment and improved their lives provide support for its effectiveness.

Emphasize Personal Growth

Self-development encompasses the process of enhancing an individual's character and abilities, whether intentionally or unintentionally, to overcome various personal and professional challenges. Continuous growth is essential for human well-being and feeling fulfilled. Even though people may not always seek external validation, they still crave a sense of progress in life. Without a regular sense of self-fulfillment, one may experience negative emotions like stress, depression, anxiety, self-doubt, and a lack of confidence in pursuing new opportunities.

Recognizing the significance of self-development for mental health and overall well-being, it becomes crucial to understand how to foster personal growth effortlessly. Engaging in self-development empowers individuals to believe they can achieve more in their careers and lives. On the other hand, neglecting personal growth may lead to feeling stuck, dissatisfied with achievements, and lacking a sense of purpose in life.

In contrast, by pursuing self-development, one can break free from stagnation, comfort zones, and accepting the status quo. It promotes growth and happiness, not only benefiting the individual but also positively impacting those around them. Therefore, nurturing personal growth is a key factor in leading a fulfilling and meaningful life.

Take Action Without Delay

If you desire positive changes in your life, start by changing yourself first. Raise your expectations and commit to lasting transformation. Embrace uncertainty as an opportunity to learn and grow. Mere interest in change is insufficient; you must plan and dedicate yourself to the journey of self-development. Utilize your existing knowledge and build upon it, or be willing to start from scratch to acquire the necessary skills.

Progress At Your Own Pace

Even slow progress is significant progress. Break your goals into smaller, achievable steps, allowing you to measure your accomplishments along the way. These micro-goals provide clarity and motivation, propelling you towards substantial self-development. The more milestones you conquer, the less likely you'll be to give up. Achieving smaller goals creates momentum and makes your larger aspirations feel within reach.

Learn From Diverse Sources

Continuous learning is vital for growth. Acknowledge that there is always room for improvement. Observe and learn from others, without judgment, to avoid repeating their mistakes. Seek inspiration from those who have achieved what you aspire to accomplish. Identify your weaknesses and focus on developing areas that need improvement. Remember the adage: "You are the average of the five people you spend the most time with."

Embrace Change Wholeheartedly

Comfort can lead to stagnation. To grow, welcome change without resistance. Avoid complacency and lead a dynamic life. Embrace change in your surroundings, relationships, experiences, and habits. You need not make drastic changes all at once; gradual improvements can be equally transformative. Assess your skills and traits, and work on improving those that require development. Openness to change is a simple yet powerful way to evolve.

Embrace Personal Accountability

Take ownership of your life and where you stand today. You are solely responsible for your decisions and actions in pursuit of your goals. Whether it's career advancement or personal growth, the outcome depends on your commitment. Many people fail to achieve their aspirations due to a lack of accountability. Instead of blaming others, look inward and acknowledge your role. It might be uncomfortable, but it's the first step toward progress.

Cultivate Gratitude and Self-Acceptance

Amidst the constant desire for more, pause and appreciate what you already have. Gratitude and self-love are essential, even for those who seem content. Society's filtered standards can lead to self-doubt and a failure to accept oneself. Recognize your blessings and embrace self-love to stay grounded and motivated. This mindset enriches your journey toward success, making your goals even more fulfilling.

Set Purposeful Intentions and Stand Out

Your intentions shape your reality. Set clear and positive intentions, and you'll find yourself on the path to success. Avoid making excuses, work hard, and take action aligned with your intentions. Excuses hinder progress, so eliminate them from the outset. By aligning intentions and actions, you'll make significant progress toward your goals.

Face Challenges and Conquer Fears

If your goals seem daunting, break them into smaller, achievable steps. Regardless of your dream's size, proper planning and effort can lead to its realization. Don't delay or wait for a better time; seize the present to pursue your ambitions. Challenge yourself and confront your fears. Overcome self-imposed limitations and take bold action. Without constraints, your path will be clear, and you'll be closer to your aspirations.

Nurture Unwavering Passion for Your Dreams

Passion holds immense power. It bridges the gap between your desires and your determination to achieve them. Without passion, goals lose their meaning and become futile pursuits. It's challenging to commit to something you don't genuinely love. Daily efforts towards your objectives will lack vigor if passion is absent. Surround yourself with supportive individuals who align with your growth-oriented mindset and goals. Living with passion infuses fulfillment and success into your life, regardless of possessions or unmet goals. Embrace passion to propel yourself into the future while relishing the journey.

Persevere and Believe in Yourself

Never give up on yourself, no matter what obstacles arise. While quitting on others may be forgivable, giving up on yourself is detrimental. It can cause mental harm and hinder your progress indefinitely. It limits your ability to envision a better, brighter future and stunts your self-development. Instead of viewing failures as setbacks, shift your perspective to see them as learning experiences. Embrace failure as a stepping stone to growth. When you cultivate resilience and welcome challenges, you'll find the strength to persist and build unshakable character.

Nurturing Leadership Skills: A Journey of Dedication

Leadership qualities may come naturally to some individuals, while others must invest additional effort to develop them. Regardless of whether leadership is an innate trait, cultivating these skills demands unwavering dedication and hard work. The process of developing leadership can be compared to mastering an art form, but it is by no means an easy path. It involves confronting challenges, embracing responsibility for others, and grappling with the consequences of one's decisions. A true leader must display diligence and remain committed to both their team and their objectives, requiring a well-crafted character that aligns with the demands of leadership.

Taking up a leadership position means assuming accountability not only for oneself but also for the actions of others. Achieving excellence as a leader entail setting high standards and continuously improving one's skills. However, the journey towards effective leadership is not without its struggles, and embracing failures becomes crucial for personal growth. Focusing solely on mistakes without seeking self-improvement will impede progress and demotivate the team.

To advance as a leader, one must strike a balance between being selfless and prioritizing personal development. Being there for others necessitates being there for oneself first. Although natural talent can contribute to leadership, continued career growth requires honing technical expertise and maintaining an unwavering commitment to personal growth and the pursuit of objectives.

7 Ways to Develop Leadership Skills

● **Cultivate Self-Discipline:**

Self-discipline involves the practice of adhering to rules and forming habits to achieve goals or tasks. It also encompasses controlling emotions and overcoming weaknesses. For effective leadership, possessing both discipline and self-discipline is essential. A leader without discipline cannot excel in their role, and lacking self-discipline can hinder fulfilling daily responsibilities. Being a leader requires being a positive example for others and inspiring them to perform at their best. To develop leadership skills, establishing a routine, such as a morning routine, is recommended to enhance organization and success.

● **Embrace Learning and Followership:**

Although leaders are expected to lead, learning from others and being open to different perspectives is crucial for developing leadership skills. Avoid stagnation by continuously learning and valuing others' opinions, regardless of their position. Welcoming diverse viewpoints fosters respect and trust within the team and paves the way for personal growth and successful leadership.

● **Undertake Diverse Projects:**

As a leader, challenging yourself with various projects beyond your current responsibilities demonstrates a growth-oriented mindset. Embracing new opportunities, character development, and taking initiative can lead to a more fulfilling career and open doors for further achievements.

● **Inspire and Empower:**

Effective leadership involves inspiring and supporting the team. Motivated and empowered team members are more likely to go above and beyond to achieve common goals. Establishing trust and valuing team members' contributions is pivotal for fostering a dedicated and high-performing team, ultimately benefiting the leader and the entire organization.

● **Foster Situational Awareness:**

To become an effective leader, it is essential to develop situational awareness, which involves the ability to anticipate potential outcomes, avoid mistakes, and gain a broader perspective. By honing this skill, leaders can adeptly navigate various situations, even complex ones, by proactively solving problems and seizing overlooked opportunities. Successful development of situational awareness can garner trust, respect, and recognition from others.

● **Embrace Continuous Learning:**

Leaders should adopt a mindset of continuous learning, seeking knowledge from diverse sources and remaining open to new ideas. Avoid complacency and the assumption that one already knows everything. Instead, evolve and sharpen the mind by exploring new methods and possibilities. A humble leader reads extensively, studies others' success, and actively learns from their team members.

● **Handle Conflict with Empathy and Listening:**

A good leader refrains from initiating or instigating conflicts for personal gain. Instead, they learn to understand and address interpersonal conflicts with empathy and effective communication. Ignoring or avoiding conflict does not promote growth or resolution. By fostering harmony and resolving potential conflicts early in the work environment, a leader can build a strong and united team, working together towards a common goal. Teaching team members to respect one another is an essential preventative measure against potential conflicts.

Mastering Effective Communication

Why is it crucial to acquire the skill of communication?

While we may all speak and understand how to articulate words verbally, the question remains: are we truly communicating effectively?

Effective communication involves the successful transfer of information to others through both verbal and non-verbal cues. As you've discovered, your body language speaks volumes about what you are conveying verbally, expressing your intentions or reservations. For instance, lack of eye contact during a conversation may signal disinterest to the other person.

In the absence of effective communication, relationships, whether personal or professional, can face significant challenges. Failure to communicate with those close to you can lead to difficulties in maintaining healthy bonds. Similarly, a lack of communication in the workplace can result in misinterpretations and decreased productivity.

To cultivate thriving relationships in both personal and professional realms, it is essential to invest effort in refining your communication skills. Each relationship is unique and requires attentive understanding. By working on enhancing communication in each of your connections, you will gain insights into what can potentially jeopardize them and how to avoid such pitfalls. Even if you initially feel uncertain about how to approach each relationship, you will learn from experience what actions to avoid, gradually improving your communication prowess.

Tips to Enhance Communication Skills:

The forthcoming tips will guide you in expressing your thoughts genuinely, regardless of your emotions or apprehensions surrounding communication.

- Mind the Timing: Before engaging with someone, consider your mental state, especially during initial conversations. Making a positive first impression is vital, and being misunderstood at work can be detrimental. Strive to be the best version of yourself and capitalize on every communication opportunity. Nonetheless, there will be days when you don't feel your best or are uncertain about what you want to say. During such times, exert additional effort to maintain a positive outlook and adopt a growth-oriented mindset. Understand that it's okay to avoid interactions until you feel ready to communicate effectively. Similarly, when dealing with conflicts, choose to discuss them calmly and patiently. Reacting impulsively to emotions is unwise; stepping away and returning with a clear mind is more constructive.
- Avoid Attacking Others; Practice Patience: Refrain from reacting based on

heightened emotions, especially when feeling angry or irritated. Instead, approach situations delicately and ensure the other person comprehends your message. If you encounter concerns with a family member, friend, or coworker with whom you generally share a good rapport, address the issue tactfully. Trusting the person, you are communicating with allows for open conversations about your feelings in a private setting.

- Embrace Honesty: Honesty remains the best policy. Embracing truthfulness in your words and actions garners respect and trust from others, who will also be more inclined to confide in you. This strengthens your relationships and brings peace of mind in all your endeavors. In contrast, those who lie often carry unnecessary worries and restrictions on what they can say. Choosing honesty enables you to lead a fulfilling life, build meaningful connections, and make ethical decisions.

- Implement the 48-Hour Rule: When someone you care about hurts or upsets you, consider discussing the matter, but if overwhelmed, wait for 48 hours. This timeframe allows sufficient space to process your emotions and gain clarity about the situation. Impulsive responses to others' actions can exacerbate hurt feelings or lead to accepting pain inflicted upon you. By taking time for self-care and reflection, you prioritize your well-being and approach communication with a composed and thoughtful demeanor.

- Engage in Face-to-Face Communication: Let's acknowledge that sending messages on our phones won't effectively resolve conflicts or facilitate proper communication. As previously mentioned, only 7% of our communication is conveyed through words alone, leaving room for misinterpretation. Opting for face-to-face conversations allows for a clearer understanding of our intended message. By doing so, we can avoid miscommunication and ensure that the person we're talking to comprehends our intentions accurately. If you're concerned about forgetting your main points, jot them down beforehand to stay focused during the discussion.

- Be Attentive to Body Language: Emphasizing body language is essential since it significantly contributes to communication. How we present ourselves and our gestures when engaging with others plays a vital role in how they perceive us. Maintaining good posture, open body language, and direct focus during conversations signals respect and encourages others to communicate more openly. Such an approach creates an environment where people feel comfortable sharing their feelings and concerns. When feeling angry, negative, or upset, take a mindful approach to address conflicts or emotions before initiating communication. Follow these steps:

- First, Pause: Avoid rushing into conversations or conflicts impulsively. Sometimes, stepping away from the discussion is the healthiest option for any relationship. For instance, during an argument with a partner, continuing the altercation may lead to hurtful and irrational statements. Instead, take a moment to collect yourself and give the other person space for reflection. Taking a break prevents the situation from escalating further, allowing for a more constructive conversation later.

- Then, Reflect: After stepping away from the conflict, let go of negative emotions and contemplate your feelings and the other person's perspective. Focus on understanding the real issue at hand rather than merely placing blame. Once you have clarity, express your feelings in a constructive manner to salvage the conversation or relationship.

- Talk: When you've finished reflecting, find a suitable time to revisit the conversation. If you still feel angry or upset, take more time to process your emotions before engaging in the discussion. When you approach the person with a calmer demeanor, they are more likely to listen and respond respectfully.

- Finally, Listen: During the conversation, show respect by giving the other person an opportunity to express their thoughts and feelings. Actively listen to what they have to say, demonstrating your interest and care for their perspective. This approach fosters equality and allows for reconciliation, issue resolution, and the strengthening of your relationship with the person involved.

Conquering Shyness, Insecurity, and Fear

Living with shyness can lead to numerous limitations and challenges, making every day experiences more daunting for individuals struggling with it. Simple tasks like speaking up, being noticed, or engaging in conversations can become intimidating hurdles. While these experiences may seem trivial to others, shy individuals may find them overwhelming. Social anxiety or social phobia affects approximately 17 million adults due to their personality traits, and even more people grapple with shyness today (Shanley, 2020).

Although shyness may be an inherent aspect of one's personality that cannot be changed, it is possible to improve one's response to experiences and approach people and situations differently. While practice won't necessarily yield perfection, it's important to acknowledge that ideal situations rarely exist. However, our perspective and mindset play a significant role. Believing in the potential for change and growth empowers us to confront shyness, insecurities, and fears with a more positive outlook.

Overcoming Shyness, Insecurity, and Fear: Action Steps

1. Embrace Confidence: Act as if you are the most confident person in the room, and others will perceive you that way. Stop worrying about what others think and start projecting self-assurance. Even if you feel insecure or fearful, challenge yourself to face those situations head-on. By pushing through your fears, you'll realize that you can handle them and build lasting confidence. Practice confident body language, such as maintaining eye contact during conversations, to reinforce your self-assurance.

2. Engage with Others: Participate in small talk and engage with people, even if it feels uncomfortable at first. Be friendly and approachable, both with strangers and those you are attracted to. Being more approachable will lead to more interactions, providing ample opportunities for growth. Avoid dwelling on reasons not to engage with others.

3. Embrace New Experiences: Challenge yourself to try new things, especially if they make you anxious. Face your fears head-on instead of avoiding them. Join a sports team, take classes with unfamiliar people, or participate in group discussions. While anxiety may persist initially, confronting your fears will lead to gradual improvement in your interactions with the world. Embrace new experiences without overthinking or excessive planning.

4. Speak Up and Embrace Vulnerability: Force yourself to speak even in stressful situations. Don't let shyness and fear limit your voice. Remember that your thoughts and feelings are valid, and you deserve to be heard. Push yourself to engage, share, and connect with others. With practice, you can break free from the constraints of shyness and insecurity, leading to personal growth, better understanding, and openness to new experiences.

5. Cultivate Mindfulness for Self and Others: Practicing mindfulness begins with directing your focus inward and developing self-awareness. By embracing and accepting who you are, you can address any hindrances that may be holding you back from achieving your goals. It is essential to

stay present in your feelings, thoughts, sensations, and ideas without avoiding or judging them. Replacing negative thoughts and emotions with positive ones is crucial for personal growth and conquering fear. Show yourself compassion and love, as this will be instrumental in your journey of self-improvement.

In addition to being mindful of yourself, extend this awareness to the people around you. Choose your interactions carefully, avoiding those who bring negativity into your life. Instead, surround yourself with individuals who inspire and care for themselves as well as others. When your social circle comprises positive and supportive individuals, you will be more inclined to engage and connect with them genuinely. Remember, cultivating mindfulness in both yourself and your relationships can lead to more fulfilling experiences and personal growth.

Conclusion

Embarking on your personal journey is akin to an art that requires continuous practice. Being highly sensible plays a pivotal role in life, as it involves heightened sensitivity in various cognitive, emotional, and social aspects. This trait is indispensable for success in all aspects of life.

In life, errors in judgment are inevitable, but responding to these mistakes with maturity is key to counteracting their impact. Embracing failures and experiences leads to valuable knowledge that prevents repeating the same mistakes, fostering better decision-making in the future.

On the contrary, being senseless entails accepting things as they are without striving for growth or accountability. To develop as an individual, embracing sensibility is essential, which involves acknowledging weaknesses and actively seeking improvement. This mindset empowers a winning approach to personal development.

Sensible individuals avoid harboring resentment towards others and instead, channel their emotions into positive intentions. Adopting a growth mindset rather than a fixed one enhances personal growth, social interactions, and career advancement.

With a mature and optimistic outlook on life, sensible individuals set meaningful goals and take persistent action to achieve them. This mindset imbues a sense of importance and dedication comparable to daily essentials like eating or brushing teeth.

A more sensible mind prioritizes listening over excessive talking, recognizing that true learning lies in embracing new knowledge. Practicing self-control encompasses managing emotions, thoughts, reactions, and habits. Respect for others' feelings and opinions becomes a natural part of this approach, as everyone is entitled to their perspectives. Sensible individuals also learn to let go of past burdens, embracing acceptance as a means to move forward positively.

Choosing optimism and seeing the positive side in every situation becomes the primary response for sensible individuals. Even amidst struggles, the understanding that challenges are transient fosters relational intelligence and drives personal growth, leading to becoming a better version of oneself.

www.ingramcontent.com/pod-product-compliance
Lightning Source LLC
LaVergne TN
LVHW020931200726
843506LV00011B/1936